WORLD RELIGIONS

Judaism

Angela Wood

W
FRANKLIN WATTS
LONDON · SYDNEY

This edition 2008

Franklin Watts
338 Euston Road
London NW1 3BH

Franklin Watts Australia
Hachette Children's Books
Level 17/207 Kent Street
Sydney NSW 2000

For Rabbi Willy Wolff
who is a real lamb

© Franklin Watts 1999

Editor: Sarah Snashall
Art director: Robert Walster
Designer: Simon Borrough
Picture research: Sue Mennell

Religious consultants:
Lesley Prior, advisory teacher and
lecturer in religious education
Laurie Rosenberg, Board of
Deputies of British Jews
Clive A. Lawton, Jewish educator

A CIP catalogue record for this book
is available from the British Library.

ISBN: 978 0 7496 7896 8

Dewey classification 200

Printed in China

The Hebrew text on the title page reads:

"The Jews had light and gladness
and joy, and honour. And in every
province, and in every city,
whithersoever the King's
commandment, and his decree
came, and the Jews had gladness
and joy, a feast and a good day."
Esther Ch8 vs 16 and 17

Acknowledgements:

Cover photographs:Impact Photos (Stewart
Weir) (right); Magnum Photos (Abbas) (inset)

Circa Photo Library pp. 14, 18l (Barrie Searle),
28; Eye Ubiquitous p.24 (Adina Tovy Amsel);
Franklin Watts pp. 7t, 11b, 12b 15b, 18r, 21b;
Guy Hall pp. 12t, 13b, 13t, 19b; Hutchison
Library pp. 5t (Liba Taylor), 25b (Liba Taylor),
5b (John Matt), 9t (Tony Souter); Impact Photos
p.19t (Rachel Morton); Magnum Photos pp.
22t (F. Mayer), 29t (F. Mayer), 22b (Abbas);
Robert Harding Picture Library pp. 11t, 20, 15t
(Eitan Simanor), 25t (ASAP/Israel Talby), 26
(ASAP/Richard Nowitz); The Stock Market
p.23; Topham Picturepoint pp. 6, 9b, 16, 29b
(David Wells); Trip Photo Library pp. 4 (A
Tovy), 7b (A Tovy), 10 (S Shapiro), 17b (I
Genut), 27b (H Rogers); Angela Wood pp. 17t,
21t, 27t

Map p.8 Julian Baker

CONTENTS

WHO IS A JEW?

THERE IS A SIMPLE ANSWER to the question, 'Who is a Jew?' A Jew is someone who has a Jewish mother or who chooses to become Jewish when they grow up. But there are more complicated answers as well.

Judaism

For most Jews, being Jewish means following the Jewish religion – called Judaism. Religious Jews believe that there is only one God who creates everything, who has a relationship with people on earth. God speaks and listens to people through prayer.

Judaism is based on the sacred text called the Torah, which means 'teaching'. The Torah is the most important part of the Jewish holy book called the Bible. The Bible tells the story of the Jewish people. (The Jewish Bible is almost the same as the Old Testament of the Christian Bible.)

A religious Jew recites prayers from a prayer book. The prayers are usually said in Hebrew.

4

A boy raises the Torah scroll before it is read. There is a set Torah reading for every week of the year.

Cultural Jews

Some Jews are not religious, or, if they are, their beliefs about God are not as important as their sense of belonging to the Jewish people. These Jews sometimes call themselves 'secular' or 'cultural Jews' because it is the Jewish culture that matters most to them. It might be singing Jewish folk songs or eating special foods or using certain words that come from Hebrew, the Jewish language.

Zionism

For some Jews, the land of Israel is the most important part of being Jewish. These Jews are called Zionists. The word comes from the hill, called Zion, on which Jerusalem, the capital of Israel, is built.

God, Torah and Israel

For all Jews, what they do is much more important than what they believe. There are three main themes which run through all Jewish lives: God, Torah and Israel. They are like three threads plaited together.

Women pray at the Western Wall – the last remaining part of the ancient temple in Jerusalem, Israel.

THE STORY OF THE JEWISH PEOPLE

JUDAISM IS ONE OF THE OLDEST religions in the world. It is not possible to say exactly when Judaism began, but the first person that most Jews would think of as Jewish was 'Abraham our father' who lived about 4000 years ago.

The earliest Jews

Abraham lived in the Middle East where people worshipped many gods, each one ruling part of life. Abraham was convinced that everything in life is connected and so there could only be one God. God told Abraham to go to a 'promised land'. Led by God, Abraham journeyed to Canaan, where he settled with his wife Sarah and their family. They were called Hebrews. 'Hebrew' means 'crossing over' – Abraham and his family had crossed over to a new way of life.

Years later, Abraham's grandson, Jacob, was given the name 'Israel' by God in a dream. 'Israel' means 'one who struggles with God'.

Jacob had a large family and his descendants were called 'the children of Israel'. One of his sons, Joseph, ended up in Egypt as a result of a jealous feud with his brothers. Joseph became an important leader in Egypt and the children of Israel were invited to settle in Egypt.

Escaping slavery, Jews safely crossed the Sea of Reeds (the Red Sea). Sadly, their enemies drowned. (From the Nuremberg Bible, 1493.)

6

The promised land

After several hundred years, the children of Israel became slaves in Egypt. But God guided them out of slavery, led by a man called Moses, towards a land of their own. This is the most important time in Jewish history and it is remembered in Jewish culture through stories and songs.

The Jews, now a people of several thousand, travelled across the desert for forty years. During this time, God gave Moses the sacred text of Torah, and ten rules for living called the 'Ten Commandments' or the 'Ten Sayings'. Eventually the Jews arrived back in Canaan – the promised land – and called it Israel.

The Ten Commandments or Sayings which are displayed in every synagogue.

Galilee, in Israel. Jews believe that Israel is the land promised to them by God.

EXILE AND RETURN

HISTORY IS VERY IMPORTANT TO JEWS because they have lived through many difficult times and survived. Jews feel that the Jewish people will never die out.

Exile

In 70 CE the land of Israel became part of the Roman empire. The Roman leaders exiled (sent away) the Jewish people from Israel. Over hundreds of years, they spread out over the world.

By the Middle Ages, many Jews had settled in Christian countries in Europe and life for them was often very hard. They suffered a lot of anti-semitism (prejudice against Jews), but their family and community life, and faith in God, kept them together and helped them to survive.

In some countries, Jews were forced to become Christians. In other countries, they had to live in walled areas called ghettos. They were often charged heavy taxes, and forbidden to do certain jobs or to own land. They were often punished or even killed for no reason.

A map of present-day Israel. Some areas, including the Gaza Strip, Jericho and parts of the West Bank, are now in Palestinian control and the Palestinian people are hoping for their own state.

The Holocaust

Since the 18th century in Europe and the USA, Jews have suffered less official persecution. But anti-semitism still exists, and the worst case of anti-semitism took place in the 20th century.

In the 1930s, the Nazi party gained control in Germany and began

8

to oppress the Jews. During the Second World War (1939–45), the Nazis tried to exterminate all the Jews living in the countries that Germany occupied. The Nazis killed six million Jews, including over one million children. The Hebrew word for the Holocaust is *Shoah*, meaning 'whirlwind'. Jews recall the Shoah as the saddest and darkest time of their history.

Return

The Jewish people had prayed for centuries that they could return to the land of Israel, which had become the country Palestine. From the 19th century onwards, Jews began to return to the area, but many governments in the region were against Jews settling there. It was only in 1947, after the *Shoah*, that the United Nations voted that part of Palestine should become the Jewish state of Israel.

This memorial at Yad Vashem in Jerusalem remembers the sorrow of the Holocaust.

An Ethiopian Jew kisses the Western Wall in Jerusalem on arrival in Israel.

HOME AND FAMILY LIFE

THE HOME IS THE MOST IMPORTANT place in Jewish life. Many Jews believe that the original temple lives on in the synagogue and the home. At home, parents are the priests, the table is the altar and the best sacrifice to offer to God is a good heart and a peaceful life.

A girl reaches up to touch the *mezuzah* on a doorframe in her home as she passes it.

Mezuzah

Every Jewish home has a small box, called a *mezuzah*, on the frame of the front door, and on the doorframes inside, too. Inside the *mezuzah* is a copy of a prayer called the *Shema*. The *Shema* (meaning 'listen') is an important part of the Torah which is said every evening and morning (see page 11).

Learning at home

Children learn to be Jewish by doing Jewish things, such as helping to prepare for Shabbat and festivals or popping coins into the charity box. Later they learn by studying and discussing Jewish texts, particularly at mealtimes. All this happens at home – learning at the synagogue takes second place to learning at home.

Kosher food

There is nothing that Jews have to eat but there are certain foods they must not eat. Food that Jews may eat is called *kosher*, which means 'proper'. Jews may eat:

- fish that have fins and scales
- meat of mammals which have split hooves and chew the cud
- the milk of *kosher* animals
- the meat and eggs of birds that eat grain
- any edible plants

Many Jewish families read, study and discuss things together around a meal, especially on Shabbat and festivals.

The high point of *Pesach*, the spring festival of freedom, is the *seder* – a special supper at home, with songs and stories. The *seder* plate (above) holds symbolic foods.

Birds and mammals killed for food must be killed with the least amount of pain and must not be shot, trapped or strangled. Once the animal has been killed, the blood is removed from the meat by soaking, salting and rinsing. The blood is believed to contain the essence of the animal's life which should be put back into the earth.

Jews do not eat meat and milk together because of the bond that exists between a mother animal and her baby.

'Hear, O Israel, the Lord is our God. The Lord is one. Love the Lord your God with all your heart, and with all your soul and with all your might.'

The *Shema*

11

SHABBAT

SHABBAT IS THE MOST important Jewish festival. It lasts from just before sunset on Friday to just after sunset on Saturday every week. It is a day of peace and rest – no work or school, and hopefully no worries or quarrels.

After lighting the Shabbat candles, women spread the light with their hands to show joy and peace spreading over the family.

Preparing for Shabbat

Earlier in the week, Jews prepare food and clean the house ready for Shabbat. On Friday, everyone makes sure they're home in time to get everything ready.

Traditionally, the table is covered with a white tablecloth. On the table are placed: two or more candles; wine or grape juice; one or more special glasses or cups for *kiddush*, the blessing for the gift of the Shabbat; two loaves of special plaited bread called *hallah*; and a cover and some salt for the *hallah*.

The plaited *hallah*, special bread for Shabbat, symbolises the three threads: God, Torah and Israel.

God, Torah and Israel

God, Torah and Israel are the themes of Shabbat. The plaited *hallah* loaves are a symbol of these themes plaited together.

There are three phases during Shabbat and each phase has a meal. On Friday evening, the theme is 'Israel'. Friends and family relax together; the mood is lighthearted and there are songs during the meal. Saturday morning is the 'Torah' phase. There is a Torah reading at the synagogue and Jews often talk about it over lunch. In the afternoon, the theme is 'God' and the feeling is much more personal. Jews rest, read or talk quietly.

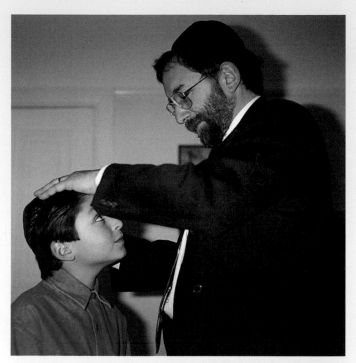

After the candles have been lit, a father says the 'priestly blessing', and some individual words as well, for his son.

'More than Israel has kept Shabbat, Shabbat has kept Israel.'
Ahad HaAm, 1856–1927

A girl sniffs sweet spices at *havdalah*.

Havdalah

On Saturday evening, when Shabbat ends, there is a ceremony called *havdalah* which means 'separation'. Jews stand for *havdalah* because they are saying goodbye to a special guest – Shabbat. It begins with lighting a plaited candle, for the three themes of Shabbat, and ends as the family passes round and sniffs sweet spices, so that the sweetness of Shabbat may stay with them.

THE SYNAGOGUE

THE SYNAGOGUE is the local Jewish community centre. In Hebrew there are three names for a synagogue to reflect its three roles: 'house of learning', 'house of prayer' and 'house of gathering'. Jews can study, pray or meet anywhere but, wherever they have settled, they have created synagogues for their community life.

Torah scrolls inside the ark of a synagogue. There is a curtain which can be drawn in front of the scrolls.

The ark

Synagogues come in all shapes and sizes. They can be a rented hall or be purpose-built with many rooms. What a synagogue needs to be a synagogue, is a special cupboard called an ark. Its Hebrew name means 'holy cupboard' and it is where the Torah scroll or scrolls are kept.

Above the ark there is always a light that never goes out. It is called the 'eternal light' and can be an oil lamp or an electric light. In synagogues which have several areas, the ark will be in the one used for prayer. When Jews turn towards the ark during certain prayers, they are usually facing the direction of Jerusalem.

Whatever the size of the synagogue, seats are usually arranged so that everyone can turn towards the ark and see at least some people's faces.

The rabbi

A rabbi is a Jewish teacher, preacher and judge of Jewish law. Rabbis conduct weddings and funerals, and are there for people in need. A congregation does not need a rabbi to lead prayers or to read the Torah, but most synagogues do have a rabbi who acts as the religious leader of the community.

Children in fancy dress attend a service at the festival of *Purim* which celebrates the biblical story of Esther.

A boy and girl read the Torah from the *bimah* during a service at the synagogue.

'The heavens above, the highest heavens, cannot contain you – how much less this house that I have built!'

King Solomon, about 900 BCE, when the first temple was built

The *bimah*

All synagogues have a platform called the *bimah*. The Torah is read from the *bimah* and many prayers are led from there. Usually, the *bimah* faces the ark and is in the middle of the synagogue, with the congregation all around. This helps Jews to feel that their prayers are coming from the whole congregation.

15

PRAYER

THE HEBREW WORD FOR PRAYER means 'examining' or 'judging yourself'. In worship, Jews believe that they can see themselves more clearly as they 'speak' and 'listen' to God.

Praying together

Jews can pray anywhere and at any time but think that it is better to pray together. That's why almost all Jewish prayers say 'we', 'us' and 'our' – and 'You' when addressing God – rather than 'I', 'me' and 'my'.

A man blows a shofar (ram's horn) calls Jews to prepare for the High Holy Day season (see page 28), a time for confession and forgiveness.

Siddur

Jews think it's really important for people to pray from the heart, but they also know how difficult this is, so there are set prayers and services. These help Jews to feel that they are not just individuals but part of a whole people, a whole story.

In Hebrew, the prayer book is called a *siddur* which means 'order'. It contains prayers from the Bible, such as the *Shema*, as well as more modern poems and hymns. Most Jews pray in Hebrew as it unites the Jewish people, but in some synagogues prayers are said or sung in the everyday language. For these Jews, it helps them feel that their prayers are part of their everyday life.

In some synagogues, men and women sit separately (children can sit with either), but in other synagogues, men, women and children all sit together.

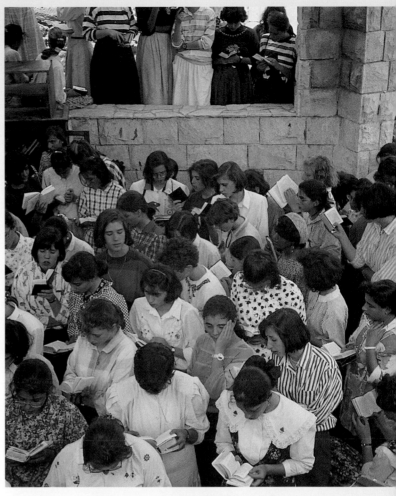

Women students, on a field trip, stop for afternoon prayers.

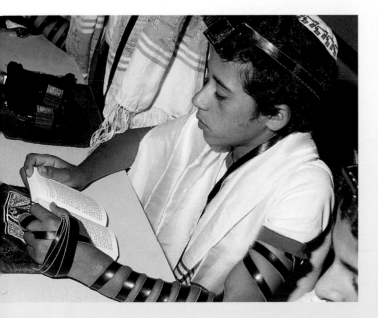

The times of prayer

Every day there are three services – evening, morning and afternoon – with an extra one on Shabbat and on some festivals. Most prayers are thanks and praise to God but some ask God to give or do something for the community or the world.

To pray, this boy wears a prayer shawl, and tefillin on his head and left arm. Tefillin are small boxes which contain part of the Torah, including the *Shema*.

JEWISH STUDY

STUDYING THE TORAH is central to Judaism. Jews study both at home and at the synagogue. The synagogue's role as a place of study is its most important role.

Study at the synagogue

Most synagogues provide a wide range of educational activities. They usually have classes to teach children and young people the Hebrew language, Jewish stories and about Jewish life and history.

Synagogues also have classes for adults. They might be about Israel or Jewish communities in other parts of the world, or about practical things like how to write Hebrew script beautifully, bake *hallah* or chant the Torah. There are often classes for adults who want to become Jewish.

Two boys unwrap a Torah scroll. Torah scrolls are wrapped in beautiful material and decorated with precious ornaments.

A *Simchat Torah* procession of all the synagogue's scrolls. A Torah scroll is always paraded before it is read.

On Shabbat and other festivals, there will often be a sermon given by the rabbi during the service at the synagogue. There will also be Shabbat study groups to discuss the week's Torah reading.

Reading the Torah

The highlight of all Jewish study is the reading of the Torah. Each Torah scroll is covered in a decorative case or cloth, with a silver plate and pointer hung around it, and silver bells or a crown on top. It is taken from the ark and paraded around the synagogue. As it passes, people bow to it or touch it with the fringes of their special prayer shawl and then kiss the fringes of the shawl. Someone removes the bells, the pointer, the plate and the cover from the Torah scroll and carries the scroll to the *bimah*. The Torah is raised in all directions so that everyone can see the text.

Rabbis and students discuss part of the Torah and other writings.

Children jump up to catch sweets at the festival of *Simchat Torah* which celebrates the end of one cycle of Torah readings and the beginning of another.

People who read from the Torah use a long pointer to follow the words. After the reading, the cover, the plate, the pointer and the bells are put back. The Torah scroll is paraded round the synagogue in the other direction and returned to the ark.

19

✡ COMMUNITY LIFE

CARING FOR OTHERS and being cared for by them is such an important part of being Jewish that it is impossible to think of anyone being Jewish by themselves. There is a Jewish saying that all Jews are responsible for each other.

'Love the stranger for you were strangers in the land of Egypt.'
The *Torah*

Jews gather in Jerusalem on Israel Independence Day, which is celebrated by Jews throughout the world.

The example of Abraham and Sarah

It is said that Abraham and his wife, Sarah, always pitched their tent near a crossroads so that travellers would have somewhere to stay. One day, after they had given a stranger a bed for the night, they discovered that he believed in many gods and was an idol-worshipper. Abraham, as a believer in the one God, flew into a fit of rage and sent the stranger away. Suddenly, he ran after him, begging him to come back. It was said that God had spoken to Abraham, saying, 'I've had idol-worshippers in my world for thousands of years. Can't you have one in your tent for just one night?'

Social activities

One of the names for a synagogue is 'a house of gathering'. Synagogues are used for many social activities such as parties, especially at festivals or at times of family celebration. After services on Shabbat or other festivals, there is usually a *kiddush* when Jews not only bless the day but also linger to chat over a drink and a bite to eat.

A girl plants a tree in Jerusalem. The Torah tells Jews to plant trees in Israel when they enter the land.

Voluntary work

Voluntary work in the community and fundraising for charities are often organised by synagogues or based in them. This work may be for individual Jews or other people, for other Jewish communities, for the people and the land of Israel, or for groups of people in their own area. Synagogues are often collection points for food and other items for refugees or homeless people.

Many synagogues run day-centres for the elderly or disabled, and toddler groups.

At a community education day, these children are making cards for the festival of *Hanukkah*.

GROWING UP

JEWS THINK OF CHILDREN as a blessing from God and there is a Jewish saying that a baby is created by three people in harmony: the mother, the father and God.

Celebrating a new birth

Soon after a child is born, the parents usually take the baby to the synagogue to announce his or her name, to give thanks for the baby and to give members of the community a chance to welcome their youngest member.

When a Jewish baby boy is eight days old, family and friends have a special ceremony called circumcision. At the ceremony, the loose skin around the tip of the boy's penis is cut away. It does not hurt the baby because, at this age, the baby's nerves have not fully developed.

Some Jews, as here, wait until a boy is three before he has his first haircut.

'Blessed is the one who comes in the name of God.'

Part of a prayer for a new born child

A boy carries a Torah scroll to the Western Wall as part of his *Bar Mitzvah*.

Circumcision is a sign forever that the boy is part of God's covenant (promise) with Israel. Afterwards, everyone says, 'Just as he has entered into the covenant, so may he also enter into the blessings of Torah, of marriage and good deeds.'

Coming of age

Traditionally, Jewish girls are thought of as adults at the age of 12 and boys at 13. From this time, they are responsible for their actions and are expected to keep the holy laws called the *mitzvot*.

To mark his coming of age at 13, a boy will lead the congregation in prayer at the synagogue, or will read the weekly passage from the Torah. He is called *Bar Mitzvah* ('son of the commandment'). Usually, there is a celebration in the family and the community.

In this century, Jews have wanted to mark a girl's coming of age, too. In some congregations, a group of girls study together and then have a special service where they read poetry and give a short talk, followed by a celebration. Usually, each girl is called *Bat Hayil* ('daughter of valour') at this time. In other congregations, boys and girls celebrate their coming of age in exactly the same way, usually when both are aged 13. The girl is called *Bat Mitzvah*, ('daughter of the commandment').

To mark becoming *Bat Mitzvah*, a girl reads some passages aloud to the congregation in the synagogue.

MARRIAGE

A JEWISH WEDDING is called 'huppah and kiddushin'. The huppah is the canopy under which the couple stand. It is a symbol of the openness and hospitality of their home. *Kiddushin* means 'holiness' – marriage is a special relationship and the couple are holy for each other.

The wedding party stands under the *huppah*. Wherever possible the *huppah* is outside.

'Blessed are you, the Eternal our God, ruler of the universe, who created joy and happiness, bridegroom and bride, love and companionship, peace and friendship.'

From the song of seven blessings

The wedding ceremony

There are many different Jewish wedding customs throughout the world, but the main elements are always the same. The couple must freely want to get married and there must be proof that they are getting married. For this there must be

The groom signs the *ketubah* which lists his responsibilities to his bride.

Congratulations!

two witnesses and a *ketubah*, a wedding document. The bride enters the *huppah* with a veil over her face, and then lifts it so that her husband-to-be can see her.

The bride extends the index finger of her right hand and the man places a ring on it, saying, 'Be holy to me according to the law of Moses and of Israel.' Some Jewish women today also give the man a ring and say similar words. The man gives the *ketubah* to the woman and it remains hers. It says what his responsibilities are to her and, if the couple ever separate, how he will make sure that she is provided for.

Under the *huppah* the couple drink twice from a cup of wine and, usually, the rabbi or a close friend speaks to the couple and the guests about marriage and family life. Finally, seven blessings are sung.

At the very end of the wedding the man usually smashes a glass with his foot. Most Jews say this is to remind them of the destruction of the ancient Jewish temple and the idea that, even when we are most happy, there is a touch of sadness in our lives. When they hear the broken glass, all the guests shout '*Mazal tov*!' (Good luck!)

The wedding couple are lifted up on chairs in a traditional dance at the wedding celebrations.

DEATH

THERE IS MUCH IN JUDAISM about the love of life, but Jews also see death as an important time. Jewish rituals and customs at the time of death have two main purposes: to show respect for the dead and to support the mourners.

Caring for the dead

When a Jew is dying, he or she tries to make a confession and say the *Shema* to be ready for death. If they can't, someone else may say the *Shema* for them. When they die, other Jews do not leave them alone and they usually light a candle near their head. The word for a Jewish funeral means 'accompanying', as Jews are going with the dead person as far as the grave.

Burial

At the funeral service, mourners often throw the first shovelsful of soil onto the coffin in the grave; this helps them to feel that their loved one is really dead. As people leave, they wash their hands to symbolise that they are leaving death behind and are beginning to return to the world of life.

'The memory of the righteous is as a blessing.'
Memorial prayer

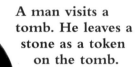

A man visits a tomb. He leaves a stone as a token on the tomb.

Mourning

For seven days after the funeral, Jews gather in the house of mourning for prayers and to share happy memories and sad feelings. Every day for a year, close mourners recite the *kaddish* – the memorial prayer which does not mention death at all but praises God as the giver of life.

On every anniversary of the person's death, in subsequent years, the close mourners recite the *kaddish* and light a candle that burns all night and day.

Men, women and children pray around the tomb of a rabbi.

A Jew lights a candle on the anniversary of the death of a loved one.

Life after death

Most Jews believe that there is life after death but they do not think about it very much and do not have a clear idea of what it is like. There is a Jewish saying which goes 'Live one life at a time!'

Jews believe that the world will end one day, and many believe that after this there will be a time of peace, love, joy, and justice which lasts for ever. There are prophecies that God will send the Messiah to make this happen and that the Messiah will be a descendant of King David.

Festivals

In all but one month of the Jewish calendar, there is at least one festival or fast. Most recall the experiences of earlier generations. The main festivals are those described in the Torah.

'In the world to come, we will have to give account of all the good things we could have enjoyed and did not.'

A saying of Rav, a 3rd century rabbi

High Holy Days

The first festivals of the year are *Rosh Hashanah* (New Year) and, nine days later, *Yom Kippur*, the Day for Atonement. On *Rosh Hashanah* the shofar is blown to call Jews to repent. On *Yom Kippur*, Jews fast and confess to God and are forgiven. In the days in between the two festivals, Jews try to make good the hurt they have caused other people.

A family sits down for a *Seder* meal. Each place is set with a silver cup, and a book called the *hagadah* for the songs and storytelling.

Pesach

There are three festivals which remember the time that the Jews left Egypt for the promised land: *Pesach*, *Shavuot* and *Sukkot*. *Pesach*, or 'Passover', celebrates the Jews' escape from slavery. On the first evening of *Pesach*, Jews have a meal called *Seder*.

Seder is both a banquet to celebrate their freedom from slavery in Egypt, and a play about their escape told through readings and songs.

Seven weeks later, *Shavuot* celebrates the Jews being given the Torah while they wandered in the wilderness.

Sukkot

The festival of *Sukkot* comes after *Yom Kippur* and is a treat after fasting and confession. *Sukkot* means 'huts' or 'shelters'. After the ancient Jews left Egypt, and before they entered the land of Israel, they wandered in the wilderness for forty years. They made temporary homes, called *sukkot* (singular: '*sukkah*').

Jewish families build a *sukkah* in their garden or on the roof of their block of flats. They take their meals in the *sukkah* and some sleep there as well. Most synagogues will have a big *sukkah* in the grounds or on the roof.

A family takes a meal in its *sukkah* during the festival of *Sukkot*.

Candles are lit in a synagogue during the festival of *Hanukkah*.

Hanukkah

Hanukkah is a minor festival that is popular among Jews in western countries. It falls in December and lasts for eight days. Each evening Jews light a *hanukiyah* outside or in the window at home. A *hanukiyah* has spaces for nine lights. One of the lights is the 'helper' which is used to light the other lights – one on the first night, two on the second, and so on. *Hanukkah* means 'dedication' and recalls the time when the temple in Jerusalem was rededicated after it had been destroyed by the occupying Roman army.

29

Important dates

BCE (before the Common Era)

c. 2000 — Abraham, Sarah and their family believe that there is only one God; they are called 'Hebrews' and feel called by God to travel to 'the promised land' to start a 'Jewish' life. They travel and settle in Canaan (Israel). Later, the Hebrews travel to Egypt where they eventually become slaves.

c. 1200 — Hebrews escape slavery in ancient Egypt after 400 years. They wander in the wilderness for 40 years where Moses, their leader, receives the Torah on Mount Sinai. They settle again in Canaan (Israel).

c. 1000 — Jerusalem becomes capital of Israel under King David.

c. 950 — King Solomon builds the first temple in Jerusalem.

721 — Israel is split into Israel (north) and Judah (south).

586 — Babylonians conquer Judah and deport Jews to Babylonia. Whilst in exile, Jews compose many writings and start synagogues for prayers and reading the Torah.

538–458 — Many Jews are able to return from exile. A second temple is built.

332 — Alexander the Great conquers Judah; Greek influence in the area becomes very strong.

175 — The Syrian Greek ruler of Judah forbids anyone to follow the Jewish religion.

167 — Successful Jewish revolt against Syrian Greek rule.

63 — Roman invasion of Judah.

CE (in the Common Era)

66–70 — Jewish revolt against the Roman occupation and abuse of the temple. The Romans defeat the Jews and destroy the temple; most Jews are driven into exile in the Middle East and Europe.

200–500 — The creation of the Talmud – a collection of rabbis' discussions and decisions based on the Torah.

600–1000 — Jewish communities prosper in Babylonia.

1066 — First Jews recorded living in England.

1095– — Christian Crusaders, travelling to recapture Jerusalem from Muslims, kill Jews in Europe on the way.

1215 — In Italy and elsewhere, Jews forced to wear a badge of identity.

1290 — Jews expelled from England.

1348 — Jews falsely accused of poisoning wells and later with killing Christians to drink their blood.

1391 — Intense persecution of Jews in Spain under 'The Inquisition'.

1492–3 — Jews are driven out of Spain and Portugal.

1516 — Turks conquer and occupy the land of Israel.

1648–9 — 'Chmilnicki Massacre' of Jews in Poland.

1654 — First record of Jews living in America.

1656 — Oliver Cromwell encourages Jews to re-settle in England.

1700 — The beginning of the Hasidic movement in Eastern Europe. This is a way of Jewish life based on the joy and love of God.

1800 — The beginning of the Reform ('modern') movement in Germany. It later spreads to Britain, USA and elsewhere.

1806 — A Jewish assembly is set up in France to show that Jews have equal rights with others under the law.

1881 onwards — Persecution of Jews in Russia. This leads to many Jews leaving for USA, the land of Israel and other countries in the years that followed.

1882 — First aliyah – migration of Jews to Israel.

1897 — A Zionist congress is formed to try and create a homeland for Jews in the land of Israel.

1933 — The Nazis come to power in Germany, leading to the Shoah.

1947 — The United Nations agrees to the creation of the State of Israel, giving the new state a small part of the ancient land.

1948 — Israeli Independence; part of Jerusalem remains in Jordan.

1967 — The Six Day War: Israel defeats the attacking armies of Egypt, Jordan, and Syria; Israel extends its territories, and reunites Jerusalem.

1980s — Increased emigration to Israel of Jews from Russia, and also from Ethiopia.

1990s — Peace agreements between Israel and its neighbours, and the beginnings of a Palestinian state.

GLOSSARY

ark cupboard containing Torah scrolls in a synagogue.

Bar Mitzvah 'Son of the commandment' – a 13-year-old boy; also the occasion to mark this stage.

Bat Mitzvah 'Daughter of the commandment' – a 12-year-old girl; also the occasion to mark this stage.

bimah raised reading desk in a synagogue.

blessing a prayer praising God; good wishes for another person.

eternal light the light over the ark.

hagadah a book of stories, songs and rituals for the *Seder*.

hallah special Shabbat and festival bread.

Hanukkah eight-night winter festival of lights.

havdalah 'separation'; a ceremony to mark the end of the Shabbat.

Hebrew the ancient language of the Jews; used everywhere for prayer and study, and as an everyday language in Israel.

huppah **and** *kiddushin* 'canopy and holiness'; the marriage ceremony.

Israel the Jewish people; the Jewish homeland.

Jerusalem the capital of Israel.

ketubah wedding document.

kaddish 'holy'; a prayer for endings and for death.

kiddush 'holy'; the prayers sung for Shabbat, over a cup of wine.

Messiah the 'anointed one' whom Jews believe God will send to bring a time of love, peace and joy – 'the days of the Messiah'. (Also spelt Mashiach.)

mezuzah small box on doorposts of Jewish homes, containing extracts from the Torah.

mitzvah **(plural:** *mitzvot***)** 'commandment'; God's wishes or laws.

Pesach spring festival of freedom and hope. It celebrates the Jews' escape from slavery in Egypt.

Purim early spring festival. It celebrates part of the biblical story of Esther.

rabbi a Jewish teacher; often the religious leader of a Jewish community.

Rosh Hashanah Jewish New Year, which falls in the autumn.

Seder a meal in the home at the beginning of *Pesach* during which the story of the escape from Egypt is told using the *hagadah*.

Shema a passage from the Torah used in evening and morning prayers.

Shoah 'whirlwind'; the Holocaust.

shofar a ram's horn, blown on *Rosh Hashanah* and leading up to it, to call Jews to repentance; also blown after *Yom Kippur* has ended.

Simchat Torah 'Rejoicing in Torah'; the autumn festival when the yearly cycle of Torah reading is ended and begun again. At the festival, Torah scrolls are paraded to singing and dancing.

Shabbat the Sabbath, a day of rest, peace and joy from Friday evening to Saturday evening.

Shavuot summer festival celebrating God giving the Jews the Torah.

Sukkot autumn festival when Jews live in a *sukkah*, a temporary home made from natural materials.

synagogue a Jewish community centre for study, prayer and meetings or social activities.

Ten Sayings also 'Ten Commandments'; ten important sayings in the Torah, from God to Jews. They are often displayed on the wall of the synagogue.

temple the place of worship in ancient Jerusalem. It has been destroyed twice and only the Western Wall remains. The worship that went on in the temple, now continues in Jewish homes and synagogues.

Torah 'teaching'; the first five books of the Jewish Bible together with a collection of ideas and values from it over 3000 years.

Yom Kippur Day for Atonement, a day for fasting and confession which takes place on the tenth day of the year. Jews remember and try to make amends for any wrongs they committed in the previous year.

Zion hill in Jerusalem. It is seen as a symbol of hope.

INDEX